THE ULTIMATE TRAEGER GRILL & SMOKER COOKBOOK 2021

Cook Delicious and Flavorful Recipes with Your Wood Pellet Grill and Save a Lot of Money with 50 Recipes

By

American Chef's Table

Table of Contents

Introduction

It is inevitable that our mouths water when we think or, better yet, when we feel the aroma of grilled meat. When we think of grills, whether it is meat, chicken, fish, or vegetables, it is very difficult not to think of a simple yet exquisite meal.

It is said that the origin of the grill goes back to 17th century France when a baron refused to pay for the iron leftover from the fence built for him by the blacksmith Phillipe Ledoux, who, in revenge, began to cook in front of the castle using the iron as support. The baron was bewitched by the smell that the meat gave off, paying the blacksmith what he owed and keeping the grill-grill.

And the aroma emitted by a grill where meat is being cooked is incomparable. Regardless of the type of food, the simple fact that it is on a hot grill makes us begin to salivate and die of hunger.

In general, grills are prepared in large gatherings where we can share with family and friends, since that is what it is all about, to share that delicious grilled meat, which takes an incomparable flavor provided by the embers and the fat of the same, along with its seasoning and its different accompaniments. The objective is to have a good time and share experiences with friends and family.

On the other hand, there are different techniques to cook food with a grill. For example, the grill consists of cooking food quickly over high heat, while the barbecue involves slow cooking with indirect and low heat for a long time, even several hours, which makes the meat more tender and better concentrates the flavors of the food.

In this sense, the Traeger Grill and Smoker, has been a great invention to facilitate the task of cooking on the grill, including functions for different cooking methods to suit every need and a particular type of food, making it possible to barbecue, grill, braise, smoke, roast, and bake. It can also adapt from low and slow to high and fast cooking, bringing simplicity and ease to wood-fired cooking.

The Traeger Grill and Smoker is an electronic grill that uses wood pellets as fuel, runs on electricity, and has multiple functions for cooking in different ways. The purpose of using wood pellets is to give food a better flavor than it would have with a gas grill. This gives any food an unparalleled flavor, whether it is beef, poultry, pork, lamb, seafood, or any vegetable. The Traeger grill is very versatile, one can prepare anything from savory foods to desserts, reaching new levels with each dish.

That's why with this cookbook you will be able to try delicious recipes that will leave everyone impressed and mouthwatering! Don't wait any longer to prepare some of these recipes!

Chapter 1: Traeger Grill Appetizers, Sides & Snacks

1. Traeger Grilled Brussels Sprouts

(Ready in about: 35 minutes | Serving: 4 | Difficulty: Easy)

Nutrition per serving: Kcal 153 | Fat 10 g | Net Carbs 5g | Protein 011 g

Ingredients

- 1/2 teaspoon of salt

- 1 cup of bacon, reserve the fat

- 1/2 teaspoon of pepper

- 2 cups of Brussels sprouts

Instructions

1. Cook the bacon crispy on the stovetop, and reserve the fat.

2. Crumble the bacon into pieces.

3. Clean and trim the Brussel sprout and cut in half.

4. In a safe grill pan, add ¼ cup of fat(bacon) on medium flame.

5. When bacon fat is hot, add Brussel sprouts 1/2 side down and sprinkle salt and pepper; let it brown for 3 to 4 minutes.

6. Let the grill to preheat 350-375 °F. Place the pan on the grill and cook for 18-20 minutes.

7. Serve hot.

2. Traeger Grilled Carrots

(Ready in about: 25 minutes | Serving: 6 | Difficulty: Easy)

Nutrition per serving: Kcal 250 | Fat 25 g | Net Carbs 6g | Protein 1 g

Ingredients

- 1/2 teaspoon of black pepper

- 1/2 teaspoon of salt

- 1 tablespoon of olive oil

- Fresh thyme

- 1/4 cup of butter

- 2 cups of large carrots

Instructions

1. Wash and pat dry the carrots and do not peel.

2. Drizzle with olive oil. Sprinkle salt to the carrots.

3. Let the grill preheat to 350 °F.

4. Put carrots directly on the grill. Close the lid.

5. Cook for 20 minutes.

6. Meanwhile, in a pan, melt butter on medium flame. Do not burn the butter.

7. Slightly brown the butter.

8. Take carrots on a serving plate, drizzle black pepper, and browned butter. Top with fresh thyme.

3. Traeger Funeral Potatoes

(Ready in about: 70 minutes | Serving: 8 | Difficulty: Easy)

Nutrition per serving: Kcal 403 | Fat 37 g | Net Carbs 14 g | Protein 4 g

Ingredients

- 1/2 cup of grated cheddar cheese

- 1 can of cream chicken soup

- 1/4 cup of melted butter

- 3 cups of corn flakes (crush slightly)

- 1 cup of sour cream

- 1 32-ounce package of hash browns, frozen

- 1 cup of mayonnaise

Instructions

1. Let the grill preheat to 350 °F, take a 13 by 9″ baking pan, and spray oil on it.

2. In a bowl, combine all ingredients except for butter and corn flakes.

3. Add this mixture into the prepared baking pan.

4. Mix the melted butter with corn flakes.

5. Add corn flakes mix on top of the hash brown mix.

6. Grill for 1 and 1/2 an hour at 350 °F until hash brown is soft.

7. Cover with foil if the top browns too much.

8. Serve hot.

4. Lemon Garlic Grilled Asparagus in Foil

(Ready in about: 25 minutes | Serving: 4 | Difficulty: Easy)

Nutrition per serving: Kcal 59 | Fat 4 g | Net Carbs 6 g | Protein 2 g

Ingredients

- 2 cups of asparagus, cleaned and trimmed

- 1 tablespoon of olive oil

- Salt and black pepper, to taste

- 3 cloves of minced garlic

- Lemon zest: One teaspoon

- 2 tablespoons of lemon juice

Instructions

1. Let the grill preheat to medium (325 °F) heat.

2. In a bowl, add asparagus and lemon juice, garlic, olive oil — coat well and season with salt and pepper.

3. Place asparagus into two different foil sheets, 1/2 in 1 and 1/2 in another. Wrap tightly.

4. Place foil packets on the grill and cook for 10-20 minutes, or until tender.

5. Grilled Garlic Rosemary Smashed Potatoes

(Ready in about: 1 hour | Serving: 8 | Difficulty: Easy)

Nutrition per serving: Kcal 287 | Fat 12 g | Net Carbs 23 g | Protein 7.8 g

Ingredients

- 2 tablespoons of olive oil

- 6 cups of small red potatoes

- 3/4 teaspoon of salt

For grilling:

- 1 tablespoon of chopped, fresh rosemary

- 2 cloves of minced garlic

- 3 tablespoons of olive oil

- 1/4 teaspoon of garlic salt

- Grated Parmesan cheese, as needed

- 1/4 teaspoon of black pepper

Instructions

1. Let the grill preheat to 375 °F. Prepare a baking dish with parchment paper.

2. Pat dry the potatoes. Coat the potatoes with 2 tablespoons of oil, and sprinkle salt. Place on a baking sheet.

3. Bake until fork-tender or for 40-50 minutes. Cool them completely.

4. In a bowl, add black pepper, chopped fresh rosemary, olive oil, salt, and garlic salt.

5. Smash the potatoes of ¾ inch thickness.

6. Brush the potatoes with oil. And sprinkle with seasoning — grill for 10 minutes.

7. Top with cheese and serve.

Chapter 2: Traeger Grill Pork Recipes

6. Pulled Pork Enchiladas with Smoke-Roasted Red Sauce

(Ready in about: 60 minutes | Serving: 8 | Difficulty: Medium)

Nutrition per serving: Kcal 345 | Fat 32 g | Net Carbs 16 g | Protein 20 g

Ingredients

- 1 head bulb of garlic
- 3 cups of pulled pork
- 3 cups of fresh tomatoes
- 1 onion
- 2 tablespoons of chili powder
- Hot pepper sauce, to taste
- 1 cup of Monterey Jack cheese, shredded
- 1/4 cup of enchilada sauce
- 8 tortillas, whole flour
- 2 teaspoons of cumin

Instructions

1. Set the Traeger to high (450 °F) and close the lid for 15 minutes.
2. Cut the top of the garlic bulb and wrap it in foil. Add tomatoes, onion sliced in 1/2 wrapped garlic on the grill.
3. Let it cook until the garlic has softened, or for 10 to 15 minutes. Raise the temperature to 375 °F and close the lid.
4. Unwrap the garlic, add tomatoes, onion, and garlic to the blender.
5. Add hot sauce, chili powder, salt, and cumin to the blender.

6. Pulse on high until creamy. If the sauce is thick, add a few tablespoons of water.

7. In a baking dish (9 by 13), spread a thin layer of prepared sauce.

8. In a bowl, add pulled pork and mix with ¼ cup of sauce. Mix to combine.

9. In each tortilla, add 1/3 cup of pulled pork and some cheese.

10. Wrap the tortillas and place them in a baking dish.

11. Cover with cheese and the rest of the sauce.

12. Place the baking dish on the grill grate and bake for 25 minutes, or until cheese is melted and sauce is bubbly.

13. Serve hot.

7. Exquisite Ribs

(Ready in about: 6 hours and 20 minutes | Serving: 5-6 | Difficulty: Medium)

Nutrition per serving: Kcal 234 | Fat 24 g | Net Carbs 12 g | Protein 26 g

Ingredients

- 1 tablespoon of granulated onion
- 1/4 cup of kosher salt
- 1 teaspoon of chipotle powder
- 4 tablespoons of mild chili powder
- 1 tablespoon of ground cumin
- 1 tablespoon of granulated garlic
- 1 tablespoon of coarse black pepper
- 1/2 cup of brown sugar
- 1 tablespoon of ground coriander
- 3 cups of apple juice

Instructions

1. In a bowl, add all ingredients, mix well.
2. Rub this mixture on both sides of the ribs. Marinate overnight.
3. Let the Traeger preheat to 200 °F.
4. Make a pan of foil, place over grill add apple juice to it.
5. Place ribs on the grill, and cook for 5 hours.
6. If you want moist ribs after every 15 minutes, brush the apple juice over the ribs. Or skip this step if you want dry ribs.
7. Close the lid and cook for 1 more hour.
8. Serve hot.

8. Pork Tenderloin Wrapped in Fresh Rosemary

(Ready in about: 60 minutes | Serving: 8-9 | Difficulty: Medium)

Nutrition per serving: Kcal 244 | Fat 16 g | Net Carbs 13 g | Protein 25.5 g

Ingredients

- 1-1.5 pounds of pork tenderloin
- 1 tablespoon of Dijon mustard
- 1 tablespoon of olive oil
- 4 cloves of minced garlic
- 3 or 4 sprigs of fresh rosemary
- 1/4 teaspoon of black pepper

Instructions

1. Let the grill preheat to 375 °F.
2. In a bowl, mix black pepper, olive oil, crushed garlic, and Dijon mustard to make a paste.
3. Spread this mixture all over the tenderloin.
4. Cut food string into 10 inches' pieces.
5. Place string two inches apart. Place 3-4 sprigs of herb across strings.
6. Place coated tenderloin over herbs and strings. Tie the strings and place the rest of the springs.
7. Trim the strings if in excess.
8. Place the tied tenderloin in the middle rack and close the lid.
9. Cook for 10-15 minutes. Turn the tenderloin over and grill for another 10-15 minutes. Cook until the internal temperature reaches 145 °F.
10. Let it rest for 5 minutes, then remove the herbs and string.
11. Slice and serve.

9. Slow Smoked Pulled Pork

(Ready in about: 8-10 hours and 15 minutes | Serving: 8-9 | Difficulty: Hard)

Nutrition per serving: Kcal 312 | Fat 17 g | Net Carbs 10.1 g | Protein 16.5 g

Ingredients

- 1 pork shoulder of 7-8 pounds, rinsed and trimmed
- 1 tablespoon of kosher salt
- 2 tablespoons of Dijon mustard
- 1 teaspoon of chipotle powder
- 1 tablespoon of garlic granules
- 1 teaspoon of thyme
- 1 teaspoon of chili powder
- Mustard based BBQ sauce
- 1 teaspoon of black pepper

Instructions

1. Do not cut the fat cap of pork.
2. Coat the pork shoulder with Dijon mustard.

3. In a bowl, add chipotle powder, chili powder, garlic granules, thyme, black pepper, and salt mix well.

4. Rub this spice mix all over pork shoulder. Place on grill and fat cap side up.

5. Smoke until internal temperature reaches from 160-225 °F.

6. Take out from grill and immediately wrap in aluminum foil.

7. Put it back on the grill until the internal temperature reaches 240 °F, slow smoke until the internal temperature reaches from 195-240 °F for 8-10 hours.

8. Remove from the grill and let it rest.

9. Unwrap and enjoy.

10. Citrus Brined Pork Roast with Fig Mustard

(Ready in about: 80 minutes | Serving: 6| Difficulty: Medium)

Nutrition per serving: Kcal 332| Fat 16.8 g| Net Carbs 11.1 g| Protein 21 g

Ingredients

- 1/2 cup of salt
- 2 tablespoons of extra-virgin olive oil
- 1/4 cup of brown sugar
- 3 cloves of garlic
- 6 peppercorns
- 1 lemon, cut into half
- 1/2 teaspoon of dried fennel seed
- 2 bay leaves, dried
- 1/2 teaspoon of red pepper flakes
- 1/2 cup of apple juice
- Icy water
- 5 pounds of pork loin
- Salt and black pepper, to taste

- 1/2 cup of orange juice
- 2 tablespoons of butter
- 1 cup of sugar
- 1 shallot, thinly sliced
- 1/2 teaspoon of minced garlic
- 1 and 1/4 cup of black figs, trimmed and quartered
- 1 cup of Cognac
- 1/2 teaspoon of Dijon mustard

Instructions

1. To make the brine, in a pot, add 1/2 a cup of salt, red pepper flakes, lemon, brown sugar, bay leaves, orange juice, garlic cloves, apple, black peppercorns, and fennel seeds.
2. Let it simmer until sugar and salt have dissolved.
3. Add this mixture over ice and keep in the fridge until cooled completely.
4. Submerge the pork in cool brine and hold the pork down with some weight if necessary. Keep in the fridge overnight.

5. Take out from brine and pat dry. Coat with oil and season with black pepper and salt.

6. Set the Traeger to high and close the lid for 15 minutes.

7. Put the pork on grill grates and cook for 20-25 minutes, at 450 °F, until internal temperature reaches 140 °F in the thickest part of pork.

8. Let it rest for 10 minutes.

9. To make Fig Mustard, in a pan on medium flame, add butter and melt.

10. Sauté shallots for 2 minutes until softened. Add garlic and cook for 30 seconds. Add sugar and cognac, let it simmer.

11. Add in figs cook until liquid is reduced to a syrupy consistency, for 20 minutes.

12. Season with black pepper and salt.

13. Pour this sauce over sliced pork and serve.

11. Crispy Pork Belly

(Ready in about: 4 hours and 15 minutes | Serving: 6| Difficulty: Medium)

Nutrition per serving: Kcal 324| Fat 18.1 g| Net Carbs 9.8 g| Protein 19.8 g

Ingredients

- 1 and 1/2 cups of chicken stock
- Dry bacon rub, as needed
- 3 pounds of pork belly
- 1 Onion, sliced thin

Instructions

- Let the Traeger preheat to 225 °F.
- Place an iron pot over grill grates and place a rack over it. Put pork belly on a wire rack and smoke for 2 hours.
- Raise the temperature to 325 °F. Put the pork belly inside the pot and cover it; cook for 2 hours until internal temperature reaches 185 °F.
- Place the meat on the griddle, put the fat side down, cook for 1 minute.
- Let it rest for 15 minutes, slice, and serve.

Chapter 3: Traeger Grill Beef Recipes

12.   Smoked Tri-Tip

(Ready in about: 2 hours and 15 minutes | Serving: 8 | Difficulty: Medium)

Nutrition per serving: Kcal 244 | Fat 13 g | Net Carb 0 g | Protein 29 g

Ingredients

- Roasted garlic blend

- 1 beef roast tri-tip

Instructions

1. Preheat the Traeger to 175 °F.

2. Coat the beef with seasoning, generously.

3. Place on grill and cook for 90 minutes.

4. Transfer to a plate cover with foil.

5. Preheat the Traeger to 400-450 °F.

6. Place the steak on the grill and cook until the doneness you want.

7. Rest it before serving.

13. T-Bone Grilled Steak

(Ready in about: 2 hours and 10 minutes | Serving: 6 | Difficulty: Medium)

Nutrition per serving: Kcal 656 | Fat 4 g | Net Carb 0 g | Protein 56 g

Ingredients

- Salt and pepper, to taste

- 2 pounds of T-bone steak

Instructions

1. Preheat the Traeger to 200 °F.

2. Place the steak on the grill and cook till the internal temperature reaches 115 °**F**.

3. Take off the grill and season with pepper and salt.

4. Sear on the skillet.

5. Let it rest for 5 minutes before serving.

14. Smoked Teriyaki Beef Jerky

(Ready in about: 4 hours + 24 hours' marination | Servings: 16 | Difficulty: Medium)

Nutrition per serving: Kcal 215 | Fat 11 g | Net Carb 2 g | Protein 22 g

Ingredients

- 1/3 cup of oil
- 1 tablespoon of minced garlic
- 1 and 1/2 cups of soy sauce
- 4 pounds of flank steak
- 1/2 cup of brown sugar
- 2 teaspoons of onion powder
- 1 cup of pineapple juice
- 1/2 teaspoon of garlic powder
- 1 teaspoon of powdered ginger
- 1/3 cup of apple cider vinegar
- 3 tablespoons of Sriracha

Instructions

1. Slice the steaks in strips with the grain.

2. In a large bowl, add all marinade ingredients. Mix well and pour in 2 separate zip lock bags.

3. Add meats in both pouches, coat well, and marinate for 1 day.

4. Preheat the Traeger to 160-180 °F.

5. Take meat strips out and pat dry. Spray the racks with oil and place strips on the racks.

6. Smoke for 3-4 hours, or until cooked to your liking.

7. The more you cook, the drier they will get.

15. Meatball Stuffed Shells

(Ready in about: 2 hours and 10 minutes | Serving: 12| Difficulty: Medium)

Nutrition per serving: Kcal 727| Fat 24 g| Net Carb 80 g| Protein 42 g

Ingredients

- 2 pounds of ground beef
- 1/2 teaspoon of garlic powder
- 8 cups of marinara sauce
- 24 shells, pasta
- 1/2 teaspoon of onion powder
- 2 teaspoons of Italian seasoning blend
- 1/2 teaspoon of pepper
- 2 cups of shredded Italian blend cheese
- 1 whisked egg
- 2 cups of shredded mozzarella cheese
- 1 teaspoon of salt

Instructions

1. Preheat the Traeger to 350 °F.

2. Cook pasta as per instructions.

3. Mix beef with all dry seasoning and egg.

4. Stuff every shell with the beef mix.

5. Place these shells in a baking pan.

6. Pour the sauce over and cheeses

7. Place the pan on the grill's top rack or on an inverted cake pan.

8. Bake for 30 to 45 minutes, until the internal temperature of the meat reaches 165 ° F.

9. Take off the grill. Let it rest, then serve.

16. Reverse-Seared Flat Iron Steak

(Ready in about: 2 hours and 10 minutes | Serving: 6 | Difficulty: Medium)

Nutrition per serving: Kcal 312 | Fat 9.1 g | Net Carb 2 g | Protein 27 g

Ingredients

- Salt and pepper, to taste

- 6 flat iron steaks

Instructions

1. Preheat the Traeger to smoke.

2. Place steak on the grill, and cook until internal temperature reaches 115 °F.

3. Take off the grill, season with pepper and salt.

4. Place on a skillet over medium flame and sear on both sides.

5. Rest the steak and serve.

17. Grilled Steak Fajitas

(Ready in about: 60 minutes | Serving: 8 | Difficulty: Medium)

Nutrition per serving: Kcal 448 | Fat 19 g | Net Carbs 37 g | Protein 30 g

Ingredients

- 2 pounds of flank steak

- 1/3 cup of light sodium soy sauce

- 2 lemons, juiced

- 2 limes, juiced

- 1 teaspoon of cumin

- 1/3 cup of olive oil

- 2 tablespoons of brown sugar

- 3 cloves of minced garlic

- 1 teaspoon of chili powder

Instructions

1. In a bowl, add all ingredients except for beef. Mix well.

2. In a zip lock bag, add beef and pour over the marinade. Coat well and keep in the fridge for 1/2 an hour or more.

3. Preheat the Traeger to 400-500 °F.

4. Place marinated steak on the grill, with the lid closed. Cook for 6-10 minutes, flip and cook for more than 6-10 minutes.

5. Take off the grill and rest 10   minutes, then serve in tortillas.

18. Grilled Mexican Style Surf & Turf

(Ready in about: 70 minutes | Serving: 2 | Difficulty: Medium)

Nutrition per serving: Kcal 543 | Fat 39 g | Net Carbs 0 g | Protein 48 g

Ingredients

- 2 steaks boneless Angus beef

- 2 8-ounce lobster tails

- 1 teaspoon of paprika

- 2 cloves of minced garlic

- 1 teaspoon of kosher salt

- Zest and juice from 1 lime

- 1 teaspoon of chili powder

- 1/2 cup of softened unsalted butter

- 1/4 cup of fresh cilantro, chopped

- 1 teaspoon of ground cumin

Instructions

1. Wash and trim lobster tails. Release the meat, and keep the tail end attached.

2. Preheat the Traeger to medium-high.

3. In a pan, add cilantro, butter, lime zest, a pinch of salt, garlic, and lime juice.

4. Cook on low heat until butter melts. Turn off the heat.

5. In a separate bowl, mix chili powder, paprika, 1 teaspoon of salt, and cumin.

6. Season the tail and steaks with this spice rub.

7. Place steaks on the grill, flip once, and cook until the internal temperature reaches 135 °F.

8. Take off steaks and let them rest.

9. Take 2 limes and cut in half, and place on grill middle side down.

10. Place lobster tails on the grill, pour over melted butter and cook until lobster temperature reaches 140 °F.

11. Serve with cilantro butter.

Chapter 4: Traeger Grill Poultry Recipes

19. Traeger Smoked Turkey

(Ready in about: 4 hours and 15 minutes| Serving: 12| Difficulty: Medium)

Nutrition per serving: Kcal 418|Fat 4 g| Net Carbs 3 g| Protein 41 g

Ingredients

- 1/4 cup of olive oil

- 1 10-13-pound turkey. rinsed and patted dry

- 1 and 1/2 teaspoons of salt

- 2 teaspoons of Traeger chicken rub

- 2 teaspoons of poultry seasoning

Instructions

1. Mix seasonings and oil, coat the turkey with this rub.

2. Rub under turkey's skin also.

3. Preheat the Traeger to 250 °F with the lid closed for 15 minutes.

4. Place turkey on the pan and put on the grill. Cook for 2 hours and close the lid.

5. After 2 hours, cover the turkey and raise the temperature to 325 °F.

6. Cook for 2 to 4 hours until the internal temperature reaches 165 °F.

7. Let it rest before slicing and serving.

20. Brined Smoked Turkey

(Ready in about: 7 hours and 20 minutes | Serving: 7 | Difficulty: Medium)

Nutrition per serving: Kcal 545 | Fat 13 g | Net Carbs 10 g | Protein 37 g

Ingredients

- 15 pounds of turkey

- Salt and pepper, to taste

- 2 tablespoons of olive oil

Brine:

- 1 tablespoon of black peppercorns

- 4 cups of hot water

- 2 cups of apple cider

- 1 tablespoon of rosemary fresh

- 1 tablespoon of steak seasoning

- 1 cup of kosher salt

- 1 tablespoon of thyme fresh

Rub:

- 2 teaspoons of dried thyme

- 1/2 cup of butter, softened

- 2 teaspoons of dried rosemary

- 1 teaspoon of black pepper

- 1/2 teaspoon of garlic powder

- 1 teaspoon of dried sage

Instructions

1. Remove neck and giblets and clean the cavity.

2. In a large pot, add all ingredients of brine mix until salt dissolves.

3. Add turkey to the brine, cover the container, keep in the fridge overnight.

4. Submerge the whole turkey add more water if needed.

5. After 12 hours or more, rinse the turkey and pat dry.

6. Put the turkey in a roasting pan

7. Preheat the Traeger to 250 °F with the lid closed for 15 minutes.

8. In a bowl, add all ingredients of spice rub.

9. Coat the turkey and under the skin too.

10. Spread olive oil on turkey.

11. Add black pepper and salt to the turkey cavity.

12. Smoke for 1/2 an hour for each pound or until the internal temperature reaches 165 °F.

13. Rest and slice.

21. Smoked Chicken Breasts

(Ready in about: 40 minutes | Serving: 4 | Difficulty: Easy)

Nutrition per serving: Kcal 135 | Fat 3 g | Net Carbs 1 g | Protein 24 g

Ingredients

- 2-3 tablespoons of BBQ chicken rub

- 1 pound of skinless, boneless chicken breasts

Instructions

1. Preheat the Traeger to 250 °F with the lid closed for 15 minutes.

2. Pound the chicken to half-inch thickness—coat chicken with rub.

3. Place chicken on smoker and smoke for 1/2 an hour, or until internal temperature reaches 165 °F.

4. Rest for 10 minutes, then serve.

22. Smoked Whole Chicken

(Ready in about: 3 hours and 10 minutes | Serving: 4 | Difficulty: Medium)

Nutrition per serving: Kcal 418 | Fat 8 g | Net Carbs 1 g | Protein 35 g

Ingredients

- 3 tablespoons of BBQ chicken rub

- 1 whole chicken

Instructions

1. Preheat the Traeger to the smoker or 250 °F.

2. Coat the trimmed chicken with a dry rub. Cover all spots and add spice rub under the skin too.

3. Place chicken on the grill and close the lid. Cook until the internal temperature reaches 165 °F.

4. Rest and serve.

23. Alabama Chicken Leg Quarters

(Ready in about: 4 hours and 45 minutes | Serving: 6 | Difficulty: Medium)

Nutrition per serving: Kcal 287 | Fat 11 g | Net Carbs 5 g | Protein 37 g

Ingredients

- 1/2 cup of all-purpose rub

- 1 bottle of Italian dressing

- 4-6 chicken Leg quarters

Alabama Sauce:

- 1 teaspoon of horseradish

- 2 cups of mayonnaise

- 1/2 cup of apple cider vinegar

- 2 tablespoons of all-purpose rub

- 1 tablespoon of sugar

- Juice of 2 lemons

Instructions

1. Trim excess skin and fat.

2. Place chicken in large zip lock bag, and add Italian dressing. Coat chicken well. Keep in the fridge for 4 hours or overnight.

3. Preheat the Traeger to 275-300 °F.

4. Take chicken out coat with rub, place chicken on grill skin side up.

5. Keep monitoring chicken so it won't burn.

6. Flip chicken after 45 minutes.

7. Cook until internal temperature reaches 170-180 °F

8. In a bowl, mix all Alabama sauce ingredients.

9. Serve with grilled chicken.

24. Chicken Lollipops

(Ready in about: 50 minutes | Serving: 6 | Difficulty: Medium)

Nutrition per serving: Kcal 243 | Fat 19 g | Net Carbs 3 g | Protein 35 g

Ingredients

- 6-12 chicken drumsticks

- 2-3 cups of Barbecue sauce

- Poultry rub, as needed

Instructions

1. Trim chicken into a lollipop.

2. Wrap the chicken bone in foil, season with poultry rub.

3. Let it rest for 1/2 an hour or 1 hour in the fridge

4. Smoke for 1/2 an hour at 225 degrees °F.

5. Cook at 350 °F for 30-45 minutes or until the meat's temperature reaches 165 °F.

6. dip chicken in barbecue sauce

7. Cook at degrees for 10   minutes, until the internal temperature reaches 175 °F.

8. Serve hot.

25. Smoked Chicken Thighs

(Ready in about: 60 minutes | Serving: 6 | Difficulty: Medium)

Nutrition per serving: Kcal 432 | Fat 32 g | Net Carbs 1 g | Protein 37 g

Ingredients

- 1 jar of teriyaki sauce

- 3 pounds of chicken thighs, bone-in

Instructions

1. In a large zip lock bag, add teriyaki sauce with chicken. Coat the chicken well.

2. Keep in the fridge for 3 hours or more.

3. Preheat the grill to 350 degrees °F.

4. Place chicken directly on grill bone side up.

5. Cook for 25 minutes with lid closed at 300 °F.

6. Flip the pieces over. Cook for another 25 minutes until the internal temperature reaches 165 °F.

7. Let it rest for 10   minutes, then serve.

Chapter 5: Traeger Grill Seafood Recipes

26. Traeger Halibut with Parmesan

(Ready in about: 25 minutes | Serving: 6 | Difficulty: Medium)

Nutrition per serving: Kcal 291 | Fat 15 g | Net Carbs 1 g | Protein 37 g

Ingredients

- 2 pounds of skinless fillet of halibut

- 1/2 cup of shredded parmesan

- 1 tablespoon of mayonnaise

- 1/4 cup of softened salted butter

- 1 tablespoon of sour cream

- 3 tablespoons of chopped chives

Instructions

1. Preheat the Traeger to 375 °F.

2. Mix all ingredients except for fish.

3. Coat the fish fillet in the cheese mix. Place on grill-safe pan.

4. Cook for 15-20 minutes.

5. Broil for 1-2 minutes, serve hot.

27. Traeger Cioppino

(Ready in about: 1 hour and 5 minutes | Serving: 8 | Difficulty: Medium)

Nutrition per serving: Kcal 711 | Fat 26 g | Net Carbs 22 g | Protein 76 g

Ingredients

Soup Base:

- 6 cups of fish stock

- 1 sliced fennel bulb

- 1/4 cup of butter

- 1 diced carrot

- 4 diced shallots

- 1 diced onion

- 5 cloves of minced garlic

- 2 teaspoons of dried oregano

- 3 sprigs of fresh thyme

- 2 15-ounce cans of diced tomatoes with juices

- 2 cups of dry white

- 1 6-ounce can of tomato paste

- 2 bay leaves

- 1 tablespoon of salt

- 1 teaspoon of red pepper flakes

Seafood:

- 2 pounds of skinless fresh fish, cut into one-inch pieces

- 2 crabs, halved & steamed

- 1 pound of prawns

- 1 pound of cleaned mussels

- 1 pound of cleaned steamer clams

Instructions

1. Preheat the Traeger to 375 °F.

2. In a Dutch oven, add butter on medium flame. Add in diced carrot, a sliced fennel bulb, shallots, and diced onion.

3. Sauté for 2 to 3 minutes, till the vegetables softened.

4. Add garlic and sauté for 30 seconds.

5. Add tomatoes with juice, herbs, fish stock, seasonings, and tomato paste. Let it simmer.

6. Place Dutch oven on the grill, let it simmer for 15 minutes until the stew's internal temperature reaches 180 to 211 °F.

7. Add all seafood.

8. Cook for 10 minutes.

9. Serve hot.

28. Blackened Catfish Tacos

(Ready in about: 25 minutes | Serving: 5 | Difficulty: Medium)

Nutrition per serving: Kcal 515 | Fat 27 g | Net Carbs 21 g | Protein 46 g

Ingredients

- All-purpose rub

- 1 pound of catfish:

- 1 cup of shredded cabbage

- 5 tortillas

- Lemon cut into wedges

- 1 cup of shredded cheese

Tartar Sauce

- 1 cup of mayo

- 1 diced cucumber

- 3 tablespoons of wasabi paste

- Juice from 2 lemons

- 1 brick of cream cheese

- 1 diced onion

- 1/4 cup of dill pickle relish

Instructions

1. Coat the fish in seasoning rub. Keep in the fridge.

2. In a bowl, add onion, cream cheese, mayo, and mix well.

3. Add in wasabi paste, 1/4 cup of dill pickle relish, cucumber, lemon juice of 1 lemon, salt, and pepper. Mix well. Keep in the fridge.

4. Preheat the Traeger to 350 °F., and place the fish on grill grates. Cook on one side for 10 minutes.

5. Take off grill and serve in tacos with tartar sauce, cabbage and. cheese

29. Traeger Honey Garlic Salmon

(Ready in about: 25 minutes | Serving: 6| Difficulty: Medium)

Nutrition per serving: Kcal 619 | Fat 36 g | Net Carbs 17 g | Protein 49 g

Ingredients

Sauce:

- 3 tablespoons of butter

- 3 tablespoons of soy sauce

- 1/3 cup of honey

- 2 tablespoons of white wine

- 2 tablespoons of minced garlic

- 3 tablespoons of balsamic vinegar

Salmon:

- Olive oil

- 6 small salmon filets

- Garlic powder

- Salt and pepper

- Onion powder

Instructions

1. Preheat the Traeger to 350 °F

2. In a bowl, add all ingredients of the sauce.

3. Pour this mix into a grill-safe dish

4. Coat salmon with olive oil and sprinkle with seasoning; place salmon in foil pan.

5. Place both pans on the grill and cook for 10-20 minutes or until salmon's internal temperature reaches 145 °F.

6. Cook the sauce for 10 minutes. Do not burn.

7. Take both pans out of the grill.

8. Pour sauce over salmon and serve.

30. Traeger Lobster Rolls

(Ready in about: 15 minutes | Serving: 4 | Difficulty: Easy)

Nutrition per serving: Kcal 234 | Fat 16 g | Net Carbs 16 g | Protein 8 g

Ingredients

- 4 rolls

- 4 lobster tails, grilled but cooled down

- 2 tablespoons of lemon juice

- 1 teaspoon of kosher salt

- 2 tablespoons of chopped parsley

- 1 tablespoon of chopped green onion

- 1 stalk of celery stalk, chopped

- 1/4 cup of mayo

- 1/2 teaspoon of ground black pepper

Instructions

1. In a bowl, add parsley, lemon juice, mayo, green onions, salt, celery, and black pepper mix well. Let it rest for 5-10 minutes.

2. Remove shells from lobster and cut into small pieces

3. Slowly mix the sauce and lobster and the sauce.

4. Toast the buttered buns in a pan. Place lobster and mixture on top.

5. Smoke in Traeger for 10 minutes at 250 °F until heated through.

6. Serve right away.

31. Traeger Spicy Fried Shrimp

(Ready in about: 35 minutes | Serving: 6 | Difficulty: Medium)

Nutrition per serving: Kcal 327 | Fat 17 g | Net Carbs 18 g | Protein 24 g

Ingredients

- 1/3 cup of oil

- 1 pound of shrimps, peeled and deveined

- 2 tablespoons of Nashville hot rub

- 1/2 teaspoon of onion powder

- 1 tablespoon of paprika

- 1 cup of flour

- 4 whole eggs

- 1/4 teaspoon of white pepper

- 1 teaspoon of salt

- 1/2 teaspoon of garlic powder

Instructions

1. Preheat the Traeger to 400 °F.

2. Pat dry the shrimps.

3. In a bowl, add all dry ingredients, mix well.

4. In a bowl, add eggs and whisk.

5. Coat shrimps in flour, then in the dry spice mix, then in egg wash, back again in flour.

6. Thread breaded shrimps on skewers.

7. Keep in the fridge for 15-20 minutes.

8. Place skewers on an oiled grill cook for 3 minutes with the lid closed.

9. Take off grill and brush with oil place again on grill cook for 5 minutes.

10. Serve hot

32. Traeger Tuna Melt Flatbread

(Ready in about: 20 minutes | Serving: 6 | Difficulty: Easy)

Nutrition per serving: Kcal 321 | Fat 15 g | Net Carbs 12 g | Protein 23 g

Ingredients

- 6 flatbreads

- 2 cans of water-packed tuna

- 1/4 teaspoon of garlic powder

- 1/2 teaspoon of salt

- 1/4 teaspoon of onion powder

- 1/2 cup of mayo

- Microgreens

- 3 tablespoons of chopped dill pickles

- 1/4 teaspoon of pepper

- 2 cups of shredded cheese

Instructions

1. Mix all ingredients.

2. Let the Traeger preheat to smoke (180 °F).

3. Place on 6 flatbreads and smoke for 10 minutes in Trager

4. Put microgreens on top

5. Serve and enjoy.

Chapter 6: Traeger Grill Lamb Recipes

33. Ground Meat Kebabs

(Ready in about: 50 minutes | Serving: 2-4 | Difficulty: Easy)

Nutrition per serving: Kcal 154 | Fat 9 g | Net Carbs 12 g | Protein 18.4 g

Ingredients

- 1 and a half-pound of chilled ground lamb

- 2 cloves of minced garlic

- 1 teaspoon of salt

- 3 tablespoons of chopped cilantro

- 1/4 cup of minced onion

- 1 tablespoon of fresh mint

- 1 tablespoon of ground cumin

- 1/4 teaspoon of ground cinnamon

- 1 teaspoon of paprika

- 1/2 teaspoon of ground coriander

- Pita bread, for serving

Instructions

1. In a bowl, add all ingredients. Mix well and shape into balls.

2. Thread meatballs on a skewer. With cold washed hands shaped into kebabs.

3. Keep in the fridge covered for 1/2 an hour or overnight.

4. Preheat the grill to 350 °F. Keep the lid closed for 10 minutes.

5. Grill kebabs for 1/2 an hour or until the internal temperature of the kebab reaches 160 °F.

6. Serve with pita bread.

34. Braised Lamb Shank

(Ready in about: 4 hours | Serving: 4| Difficulty: Medium)

Nutrition per serving: Kcal 324 | Fat 14 g | Net Carbs 10 g | Protein 22 g

Ingredients

- 4 lamb shanks, whole

- 4 sprig fresh thyme and rosemary

- Traeger Prime rib rub

- 1 cup of red wine

- 1 cup of beef broth

Instructions

1. Coat the Lamb with prime rib rub.

2. Let the Traeger preheat to 500 °F, keep the lid closed for 15 minutes.

3. Put coated lamb shanks on the grill and cook for 20-25 minutes.

4. Place the grilled shank in a Dutch oven. Add in herbs, beef broth, and wine. Cover tightly and place on the grill again at 325 °F.

5. Let it cook for 3-4 hours until the meat thickest part internal temperature reaches 180 °F.

35. Lamb Wraps BBQ Style

(Ready in about: 3 hours | Serving: 4| Difficulty: Medium)

Nutrition per serving: Kcal 314| Fat 19 g| Net Carbs 18.9 g| Protein 23 g

Ingredients

- Juice from 1 lemon

- Traeger Big game rub

- 1 lamb leg

- 1 red onion, cut into slices

- 2 cups of Greek yogurt

- Olive oil

- 2 cucumbers

- Juice and zest from 2 lemons

- 4 tablespoons of fresh dill chopped

- 2 cloves of garlic

- 3 Roma tomatoes, diced

- 2 tablespoons of fresh mint leaves

- 12 pitas

- 1 cup of feta cheese

- Kosher salt and black pepper, to taste

Instructions

1. Rub olive oil, lemon juice on lamb leg (should be at room temperature.) Coat with a big game rub.

2. Set the Traeger to high and keep the lid closed for 15 minutes.

3. Roast lamb leg for 1/2 an hour at 500 °F.

4. Lower the temperature to 350 °F and keep cooking until the thickest part of the lamb leg reaches 140 °F.

5. Meanwhile, add the rest of the ingredients except for cheese and diced tomato in a bowl and mix well. Keep in the fridge.

6. Slice the Lamb, and place in warmed pita top with Tzatziki sauce, feta cheese, and diced tomato.

7. Serve and enjoy.

Chapter 7: Traeger Grill Vegetables Recipes

36. Roasted Broccoli Cheese Soup

(Ready in about: 2 hours and 25 minutes | Serving: 4 | Difficulty: Easy)

Nutrition per serving: Kcal 44 | Fat 5 g | Net Carb 1 g | Protein 0 g

Ingredients

- 3 cups of broccoli florets

- 2 cups of half-and-half

- 1 cup broccoli stems, cut into slices

- Olive oil

- 1/4 cup of all-purpose flour

- 2 carrots, cut into thin rounds

- 6 tablespoons of butter

- 2 cups of chicken stock

- 1 clove of garlic

- 1 yellow onion, diced

- 1/2 teaspoon of paprika

- 1/2 cup of grated cheddar cheese

- 1/2 teaspoon of mustard powder:

- Pinch of cayenne powder

- 3/4 teaspoon of salt and black pepper, each

Instructions

1. Preheat the grill to 425 °F. Cut broccoli into bite-size pieces, place on a baking tray, coat with olive oil, and season with salt.

2. Roast for 5 minutes on the grill. Take off the grill and set it aside.

3. Preheat a cast-iron skillet on the grill, with the lid closed.

4. Sauté onion with 1 tablespoon of butter for 4 minutes. Add garlic and cook for 30 seconds.

5. Transfer the mixture to a plate.

6. Lower the grill's temperature to 375 °F with a cast iron skillet inside.

7. Add 4 tablespoons of butter and flour, cook for 20 minutes, stirring every 5 minutes.

8. Add stock and whisk, then add 1/2 & half, keep mixing. Cook until thickens, or for 45 minutes.

9. Add garlic, onion and broccoli, cayenne, paprika, pepper, mustard powder, and salt.

10. Let it simmer for 20-25 minutes. Add cheese cook until melted.

11. Serve right away.

37. Traeger Grilled Vegetables

(Ready in about: 35 minutes | Serving: 8 | Difficulty: Easy)

Nutrition per serving: Kcal 44 | Fat5 g | Net Carb 1 g | Protein 0 g

Ingredients

- 1-2 tablespoons of Traeger Veggie seasoning

- 1 tray of mixed vegetables, your choice

- 1/4 cup Vegetable oil

Instructions

1. Preheat the Traeger to 375 °F.

2. Toss the vegetables in oil and vegetable rub. Place on a baking sheet.

3. Put on the grill, cook for 10-15 minutes. Serve and enjoy.

38. Roasted Carrots with Pistachio & Pomegranate Relish

(Ready in about: 40 minutes | Serving: 6 | Difficulty: Medium)

Nutrition per serving: Kcal 211 | Fat 8.8 g | Net Carb 4 g | Protein 21 g

Ingredients

- 2 teaspoons of kosher salt

- 2 teaspoons of Fennel seed

- 2 Bunch of rainbow carrots

- 1 teaspoon of sugar

- 1/2 teaspoon of cumin

- 2 tablespoons + 1/3 cups of olive oil

- 1/2 cup of Pomegranate seeds

- 1/2 cup of chopped pistachios

- 2 cloves of minced garlic

- 1/4 cup of chopped flat-leaf parsley

- 1 teaspoon of coriander

- 1/4 cup of chopped mint

- Salt

- Zest and juice of 1 lime

Instructions

1. Preheat the Traeger to 450 °F.

2. In a bowl, add all spices, garlic, sugar, salt with 2 tablespoons of olive oil. Add carrots and coat them well.

3. Roast for 1/2 an hour on a sheet tray. Take out from grill, sprinkle with zest.

4. In a bowl, add ¼ of olive oil, herbs, lime juice, salt, pomegranate seeds, and pistachios. Whisk well and adjust seasoning.

5. Serve carrots with pomegranate relish.

39. Smoked Pumpkin Soup

(Ready in about: 2 hours and 30 minutes | Serving: 6 | Difficulty: Medium)

Nutrition per serving: Kcal 315 | Fat 11 g | Net Carb 19.4 g | Protein 24 g

Ingredients

- 5 Pounds of the whole pumpkin

- 1 diced onion

- 2 cloves of minced garlic

- 1/8 teaspoon of ground allspice

- 3 tablespoons of butter

- 1 tablespoon of brown sugar

- 5 cups of chicken broth

- 1 teaspoon of paprika

- 1 teaspoon of ground cinnamon

- 1/2 cup of whipped cream

- 1/8 teaspoon of ground nutmeg

- Fresh parsley

- 1/2 cup of apple cider

Instructions

1. Cut the pumpkin into quarters and take out the seeds.

2. Preheat the Traeger to 165 °F.

3. Smoke pumpkin for 60 minutes on the grill cut side down.

4. Raise the temperature to 300 °F, and cook pumpkin until tender, for 90 minutes.

5. Take it out and peel the skin off.

6. In a large pot, melt butter. Sauté garlic, onion for 5 minutes until soft.

7. Add in all dry spices and sugar. Add apple cider vinegar cook until syrup-like and reduced.

8. Add chicken broth and roasted pumpkin. Simmer for 1/2 an hour.

9. Puree the soup in a blender, add more broth if it is too thick, and season with pepper and salt to your liking.

10. Serve with heavy cream and parsley.

Chapter 8: Traeger Grill Bonus Recipes

40. Traeger Banana Bread

(Ready in about: 1 hour and 10 minutes | Serving: 12 | Difficulty: Medium)

Nutrition per serving: Kcal 530 | Fat 22 g | Net Carbs 77 g | Protein 7 g

Ingredients

- 1 cup of white sugar

- 4 bananas, extra ripe

- 1 and 1/2 tablespoons of vanilla

- 1 cup of canola oil

- 4 whole eggs

- 1 cup of sour cream

- 2 teaspoons of baking soda

- 1 cup of dark brown sugar

- 3 cups of flour

Cinnamon Topping:

- 1 teaspoon of cinnamon

- 2/3 cup of white sugar

Instructions

1. Preheat the Traeger to 350 °F.

2. In a bowl, add all ingredients, except for cinnamon toppings. Mix with a mixer for 2-3 minutes.

3. In an oiled Bundt pan, add 1/2 of the batter.

4. Mix topping ingredients and sprinkle 1/2 on the batter. Pour the rest of the batter and sprinkle with 1/2 of the topping.

5. Place on the top rack—Cook for 1 hour. Hallway through rotates the pan.

6. Bake until a toothpick comes out a little moist.

7. Total time will vary.

8. Serve warm.

41. Smoked Baked Potato Soup

(Ready in about: 1 hour and 20 minutes | Serving: 8 | Difficulty: Hard)

Nutrition per serving: Kcal 387 | Fat 26 g | Net Carbs 31 g | Protein 9 g

Ingredients

- 1 cup of beer

- 2 cups of chicken stock

- 3 pounds of russet potatoes

- 1/4 cup of flour

- 2 cups of milk

- 1 diced onion

- 1 cup of heavy cream

- 2 cups of shredded cheddar sharp cheese

- 1 pound of bacon, slice into 1" pieces

- Scallions

- 1 tablespoon of dried thyme

- Salt and pepper, to taste

Instructions

1. Preheat the Traeger to 225 °F. Smoke potatoes for 60 minutes.

2. Raise the temperature of Traeger to 400 °F, cook until the internal temperature reaches 185 °F.

3. Cook bacon in a Dutch oven until it starts to brown.

4. Add onions, cook until turn translucent. Take out ¼ cup of it.

5. Drain the fat and leave only ¼ cup of fat in the pot.

6. Smash two potatoes and fry them. Cut the rest of the potatoes into cubes and add in onion bacon mix.

7. Add beer and deglaze the oven.

8. Add flour cook for two minutes. Add mashed potatoes and stock.

9. Add milk, cream and let it simmer. Do not boil.

10. Take off from stovetop, add in cheese until melts.

11. Turn heat on and add pepper, thyme, and salt.

12. Serve with scallions.

42. Traeger Eggnog Cheesecake

(Ready in about: 1 hour and 20 minutes | Serving: 8 | Difficulty: Medium)

Nutrition per serving: Kcal 439 | Fat 31 g | Net Carbs 35 g | Protein 7 g

Ingredients

- 3 tablespoons of melted butter

- 7 graham crackers

- 3/4 cup of white sugar

- 1/2 cup of egg nog

- 2 whole eggs

- 2 tablespoons of dark rum

- 2 6-ounce packages of cream cheese, at room temperature

- 1 and 1/2 tablespoons of vanilla extract

- Cinnamon

- 2 tablespoons of flour

Instructions

1. Preheat the Traeger to 325 °F.

2. In a bowl, mix crackers with melted butter. Press into 8" pie pan.

3. In a mixer, mix sugar and cream cheese on medium for 1 minute. Add in flour, egg nog, vanilla, and rum. Mix 1 minute. Stir in eggs and mix lightly with hands.

4. Pour batter on the crackers. Put on the grill on the top rack or on an inverted rack.

5. Bake for 60 to 75 minutes at 325 °F, until still jiggly.

6. Cool for 1 hour before serving.

43. Smoked Crumb Apple Pie

(Ready in about: 1 hour and 55 minutes | Serving: 8 | Difficulty: Medium)

Nutrition per serving: Kcal 482 | Fat 9 g | Net Carbs 70 g | Protein 5 g

Ingredients

For Pie:

- 1/8 teaspoons of salt

- 1 pie crust

- 3 tablespoons of flour

- 5 and 1/2 cups of apple slices

- 1 teaspoon of Cinnamon

- 1/4 cup of sugar

Crumb Topping:

- 1/2 cup of butter

- 1/2 cup of flour

- 1/2 cup of quick oats

- 1/2 cup of brown sugar packed

Instructions

1. Preheat the Traeger to 300 °F.

2. Place pie crust in a 9-inch pie pan.

3. In a bowl, add salt, sugar, cinnamon, and flour. Mix with apples.

4. Pour onto the pie crust.

5. Mix the topping ingredients. Sprinkle over apple mixture.

6. Bake for 1 and 1/2 hours.

7. Serve warm.

44. Smoked Strawberry Crisp

(Ready in about: 45 minutes | Serving: 8 | Difficulty: Medium)

Nutrition per serving: Kcal 471 | Fat 5 g | Net Carbs 74 g | Protein 9 g

Ingredients

For Filling

- 1/4 cup of all-purpose flour
- 6 cups of strawberries, cut into halves
- 2 tablespoons of orange juice.

For Topping:

- 1/4 cup of flour
- 1/2 teaspoon of cinnamon
- 2 cups of classic granola
- 1/3 cup of brown sugar
- 4 tablespoons of softened butter

Instructions

1. Preheat the Traeger to 350 °F.

2. In a bowl, add all the ingredients of filling — place in cast iron skillet.

3. In another bowl, mix the topping ingredients. Spread over the filling.

4. Place on grill and cook for 1/2 an hour with lid closed.

5. Serve warm.

45. Smoke S'mores Nachos

(Ready in about: 20 minutes | Serving: 6| Difficulty: Easy)

Nutrition per serving: Kcal 211 | Fat 13 g| Net Carbs 15 g| Protein 3g

Ingredients

- 1 chocolate bars

- 1 packet marshmallows

- Graham crackers

Instructions

1. Crush crackers and put them in a grill-safe pan.

2. Put broken pieces of chocolate bar on top of crackers.

3. Top with marshmallow.

4. Cook in Traeger for 10 minutes at 225 °F.

5. Raise the temperature to 375 °F — Cook for 5 minutes.

6. Serve hot.

46. Hot Dog Burnt Ends

(Ready in about: 50 minutes | Serving: 5 | Difficulty: Medium)

Nutrition per serving: Kcal 143 | Fat 6 g | Net Carbs 18 g | Protein 6g

Ingredients

- Mustard

- Poultry seasoning

- 12-15 hot dogs

- 1/4 cup of butter

- 1/4 cup of brown sugar

- 1/4 cup of BBQ sauce

Instructions

1. Preheat the Traeger to 225 °F.

2. Mix poultry seasoning and mustard.

3. Coat hot dogs in the mustard mix.

4. Smoke for 60-90 minutes.

5. Raise the temperature to 350 °F. Takes out the hot dogs.

6. Slice into 2-inch lengths.

7. Place in 9 by 13" pan.

8. In a bowl, add butter, BBQ sauce, and brown sugar. Mix well.

9. Pour over hot dogs and mix well.

10. Place in Traeger cook for 30-45 minutes.

11. Serve with toothpicks.

Chapter 9: Dressings & Sauces

47. Cilantro Vinaigrette

(Ready in about: 10 minutes | Serving: 2| Difficulty:
Easy)

Nutrition per serving: Kcal 40| Fat 3 g| Net Carbs
2g| Protein 0.1 g

Ingredients

- 2 tablespoons of fresh lime juice

- 1 and 1/2 tablespoons of extra virgin olive oils

- 2 tablespoons of minced cilantro

- 1/2 teaspoon of agave nectar

- 1/4 teaspoon of kosher salt

- 1 clove of minced garlic

Instructions

1. In a bowl, add all the ingredients.

2. Whisk them well.

3. Keep in the fridge till serving time.

48. Traeger Smoked Salsa Verde

(Ready in about: 50 minutes | Serving: 6| Difficulty: Easy)

Nutrition per serving: Kcal 25| Fat 1 g| Net Carbs 2g| Protein 1 g

Ingredients

- 3 seeded Anaheim peppers

- 1 tablespoon of canola oil

- 2 seeded Pasilla peppers

- 1 seeded jalapeno

- 1/2 diced medium onion

- 6   medium Mexican husk tomato

- 3 cloves of minced garlic

- 1 cup of chopped cilantro

- Juice of 1 lime

- 1 teaspoon of salt

- 1/2 cup of chicken stock

Instructions

1. On a silicone baking sheet, place garlic, husk tomatoes, onion, and seeded peppers.

2. Let the Traeger preheat to 225 °F. Place the tray of vegetables in Traeger and let it cook for 1/2 an hour.

3. Take out from the grill and let it cool. Put all of these in a blender and pulse on high until pureed.

4. In a pan, add canola oil over medium flame. Add in the puree. Let it simmer over low heat for 10-15 minutes.

49. Jeremiah's Killer Steak Marinade

(Ready in about: 15 minutes | Serving: 6 | Difficulty: Easy)

Nutrition per serving: Kcal 164 | Fat 10 g | Net Carbs 19 g | Protein 2 g

Ingredients

- 1/2 cup of pineapple juice
- 2 tablespoons of honey
- 1 teaspoon of minced fresh ginger:
- 1/4 cup of oil
- 1/4 cup of brown sugar
- 1/2 cup of soy sauce
- 2 tablespoons of minced garlic
- 1/4 cup of white vinegar
- 1/2 teaspoon of granulated garlic
- 1/2 teaspoon of black pepper
- 1 teaspoon of onion powder

Instructions

1. In a bowl, add all the ingredients, whisk until sugar is well combined.

2. Marinate the steaks or reduce on low heat and serve with cooked steaks.

50. Alabama Sauce

(Ready in about: 10 minutes | Serving: 6 | Difficulty: Easy)

Nutrition per serving: Kcal 210 | Fat 12 g | Net Carbs 16 g | Protein 7 g

Ingredients

- 1 tablespoon of sugar
- 2 cups of mayonnaise
- 1/2 cup of apple cider vinegar
- 1 teaspoon of horseradish
- 2 tablespoons of All-Purpose rub
- Juice from 2 lemons

Instructions

1. In a bowl, add all ingredients.
2. Whisk until sugar is well combined. Marinate the steaks and cook.

Conclusion

Sharing with family and friends a good and abundant meal prepared on the grill brings infinite pleasure. By sharing that delicious grilled meat, along with a glass of the wine of our preference, we can create experiences and bonds of union with other people, spend time together and have unparalleled fun. In this regard, a good barbecue or grilled meal is a reason for a family reunion, and also when organizing a family reunion, it is inevitable to think of a good grilled meal.

Although cooking on the grill requires techniques and some practice or experience, this task has been simplified by the Traeger Grill and Smoker. As a full-featured electronic grill, you can barbecue, grill, braise, smoke, roast and bake almost any food you can think of.

Nothing brings the incomparable flavor that fire and smoke bring to food. In fact, preparing food with the help of smoke is an ancient way of seasoning food, because when the smoke passes through the meat it imbues it with flavor and smell, resulting in a unique and delicious taste.

Likewise, wooden pallets, when burning, are an essential element to give that special flavor to food, so in the market, you can buy different versions of pallets in different woods that will give that special touch to the food.

When using a grill, the meat, and any food, is cooked evenly and without additives, so it retains all its properties, so we eat healthy and much richer!

CPSIA information can be obtained
at www.ICGtesting.com
Printed in the USA
BVHW041415170521
607552BV00002B/319